CAMBRIDGE

Photography: Andrew Péarce
Text: Claire Devas
Midsummer Publishing

Dedicated to Debi and Juliette

PHOTOGRAPHER

Andrew Pearce ARPS
Fotogenix

AUTHOR

Claire Devas

EDITORS

Brigid Martin
Alan Martin
Katie Collins
Sonya Larkin
Andrew Garwood-Gowers

DESIGNERS

Frances Lloyd
Debi Pearce
Alan Martin

PRINTING

BPS Group, Attleborough, Norfolk
Nick Brown, Paul Boardman, Chris Caswell

PUBLISHING

Devas and Pearce's Cambridge was first published in July 2001 by
Midsummer Publishing, 15 North Terrace, Midsummer Common,
Cambridge, CB5 8DJ England

ISBN: 0-9540635-0-3

Select photographs reproduced by kind permission of:
Phillip Mynott
J.E.T Photographic
The Masters, Principals, Presidents, Provosts, Fellows and Scholars of;
Peterhouse, Clare, Corpus Christi, Gonville and Caius, King's,
Queens', Jesus, Christ's, St. John's, Trinity, Emmanuel, Magdalene,
Sidney Sussex, Downing and Newnham Colleges.

RIGHT: *St. John's Tower and the river Cam*
PREVIOUS PAGE: *The Backs in spring*

CONTENTS

RIGHT: *Studying at Trinity*

FOREWORD

A rural market town located on a sleepy river is the home of the world's most famous university. It is a splendid melange of eirenic citizens, thousands of students cycling through the streets, and endless visitors roaming round the colleges. My only advice to them is to avoid the closed period just before examinations and to remember that in Cambridge the bicycle is king.

Cambridge has many claims to fame not least its striking beauty. Like Paris all its treasures are on show. Above all it is the centre for historical, medical and scientific research which has made it world-renowned. Cambridge minds have influenced thought for centuries but never more so than today.

This book shows the city with its history and many beauties, plethora of churches, its challenging museums housing hidden treasures. College lawns are inviting but only fellows are allowed to tread on them. The river too is quintessentially Cambridge. While Oxford paddles Cambridge punts.

Cambridge is the city that I have been delighted to be part of in different roles, as undergraduate, graduate and don, but above all as Master of Emmanuel. Emmanuel may not be Cambridge's grandest college but it is certainly its most beautiful and lively. As Master my greatest joy was the friendship of so many undergraduates, both men and women, looking forward to the future with bright-eyed expectation. They studied hard but at the same time managed to enjoy themselves. I was privileged to be able to contribute to the good of the College. The Queen's Building, a combination of theatre, music and public rooms, by Michael Hopkins is the best contemporary building in Cambridge. The old broken down boathouse was restored, and both women's and men's crews have been Head of the River. Cambridge above all is a place for love and friendship which gets crowded out later in life.

There are many entertaining stories about Cambridge, like the vice chancellor who remarked that Oxford was very lucky to come second in the boat race. There was also the American lady who looking at the Palace of Westminster said to her husband that it was Oxford or Cambridge but she was not quite sure which. This ranks with the tourist who admired Windsor Castle but enquired why on earth they had built it so near an airport.

When you are satiated with culture and architecture there are the myriad of little cafés and hostelries which provide refreshment to the body as surely as other experiences elevate the soul.

Cambridge is the Shangri-la of thousands of foreign students and they flock here year after year in search of the ideal. So whether you are studying here or spending a day or a week or a year, I hope that Cambridge will be a memorable experience and I hope also that you will enjoy this book, published by one of my star pupils, Alan Martin, and rejoice in Cambridge as much as I do. Unlike the Ritz Hotel it really is open to all.

Lord St. John of Fawsley P.C., F.R.S.L., D Litt.
Master of Emmanuel College 1991-98, Chairman of the Royal Fine Art Commission Trust, former Cabinet Minister for Arts and Culture, President of Emmanuel Boat Club

BEGINNINGS

Cambridge began as a small Roman settlement on a hill above a river. The fort served as a stopping post for travellers and Roman legions moving between the headquarter garrisons at Colchester and Leicester.

By the time the Romans had left in 400AD, Cambridge was a busy market town. During the Dark Ages, it was inhabited by both Anglo-Saxons and Danes. Its early name of Grantebryg, meaning 'great bridge', is recorded in the Anglo-Saxon chronicles in 875AD. The Danes established Cambridge as the principle town in the region when they divided England into counties. The Saxon Church of St. Bene't's dates from around 1025AD and is the oldest standing remnant of this period.

Like the Romans and Danes before them, the Norman conquerors recognised the strategic importance of Castle Hill in a county where high vantage points are scarce. They settled in the town in 1068, building a motte-and-bailey castle to combat invaders from the Fens. Several friaries and a nunnery were founded, and the river Cam - so navigable that until 1295 Cambridge was considered a seaport – continued to provide prosperous trade. In recognition of this prosperity, King John granted Cambridge a charter in 1201 awarding the town more autonomy in matters of tax and justice.

Against this backdrop, a handful of scholars, who had fled from riots in Oxford, arrived in Cambridge in 1209 and founded what has become one of the most famous universities in the world. Initially 'the University' was an organisation of teachers and scholars who lived and conducted their studies in hostels, monasteries and churches. The first college, Peterhouse, was founded in 1284, and as support was gained from the Crown and the Church, the University flourished and numerous other colleges were founded. Each new college was founded with a Master and a small number of Fellows and students. Over the centuries, the colleges replaced the hostels and all tutoring was conducted within the colleges. Lectures are now held at the University faculties, but individuals are still tutored by Fellows in the colleges. There are now 31 colleges and the number continues to grow.

TOP: *Trinity Hall milestone*
RIGHT: *Aerial view of Trinity College from St. Mary the Great*
PREVIOUS PAGE: *Trinity and St. John's Backs.*

PETERHOUSE

Peterhouse was the first of the Cambridge colleges to be founded and is also the smallest; within its intimate courts and gardens lies an easy charm.

It was founded in 1284 by the Bishop of Ely, Hugh de Balsham, who bought two houses on the site for one Master and 14 impoverished students. The College provided them with accommodation and board, and the rules required that they take oaths, wear clean surplices, and only meet with friends in respectable establishments.

The chapel was built in 1628 when the then Master, Matthew Wren, uncle to Sir Christopher Wren, demolished the existing buildings. In their place he built the library and the chapel, the façade of which has been compared to an old grandfather clock. Until that time the scholars worshipped in their local church, St. Peter's-without-Trumpington-Gate; now St. Mary the Less. This was common practice amongst colleges until they could afford their own chapel.

Tucked away behind the courts stands the old, low wall that encloses the Deer Park. Peterhouse kept deer for their supper table until the 1930s when they died out due to disease. Now the enclosure, brimming with daffodils in spring, is used for May Balls and events such as weddings and receptions. Despite the absence of deer on the menu, the College is still known for its good food and huge brunches on Sundays. Beyond the Deer Park lie the Scholars' Gardens whose landscaped paths lead down to the river and the meadows of Coe Fen.

TOP LEFT: *The Deer Park*
ABOVE: *Old Court*

Sir Frank Whittle, inventor of the jet engine, patented his idea in 1930, aged only 22, while working for the RAF. He gained such good results from the Officer's School of Engineering that he was assigned to take the Mechanical Sciences Tripos at Cambridge and came up to Peterhouse in 1934. It was during his time at the College that he and two fellow RAF officers developed the jet engine.

CLARE

The history of Clare College is peppered with false starts. Founded originally as University Hall in 1326 by the Chancellor of the University, Richard de Badew, the College was poor and possessed only two chairs; one for the Master and the other for eminent visitors. It was in financial ruin when in 1338 Lady Elizabeth of Clare took it upon herself to refound the College and duly renamed it Clare Hall. It did not become Clare College until 1856. Widowed three times by the age of 30, Lady Elizabeth was a wealthy heiress with enlightened views. She stipulated that the College should house a Master, nineteen Fellows and provide free lodging and education for ten poor scholars.

Hugh Latimer was a Fellow at Clare College and a gifted preacher with radical protestant views. During the Reformation, he gave sermons at the church of St. Edward King and Martyr, and when Henry VIII broke with the Papacy in 1534, Latimer became one of the King's chief advisors. He fell out of favour when Mary Tudor came to the throne, and in 1555 he was burnt at the stake in Oxford.

West Range from the Fellows' Garden

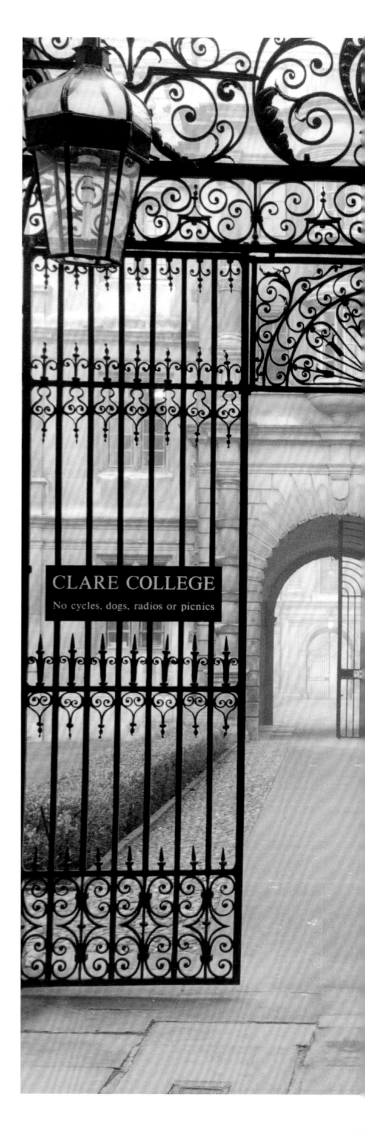

Clare College's chequered history played an important role in shaping its present day architecture. The majority of Clare Hall burnt down in 1521, and by the early 17th century, the buildings erected on the site were already considered so dilapidated that plans were drawn up to rebuild the entire College. There have been few alterations made to the main court since the 17th century, the style of which makes it easy to forget that Clare College is the second oldest of the Cambridge colleges.

Clare Bridge is the oldest surviving college bridge: built in 1638, it was the first to be designed in the neo-classical style. Of the fourteen stone balls placed upon it, one has a segment missing, supposedly the mason Thomas Grumbold's revenge for receiving a mere three shillings for his designs. Not long ago, two students made a polystyrene replica of a stone ball and to the horror of a group of tourists punting by, heaved it over the side of the bridge. As cries of panic rang out, the ball fell gently down, bounced, and floated down the Cam.

Across the bridge, through the intricate 18th century wrought iron gates, lie the secluded Fellows' Garden for which Clare College is renowned. The orderly, well-kept feel of the College extends to the garden, where plush foliage and a diversity of trees, flowers and winding paths render this one of the more romantic and intimate college gardens. During the spring, students perform plays on the lawns and around the pond.

Clare Bridge

GONVILLE AND CAIUS

Three impressive gates through the College symbolise the student's academic journey from matriculation to graduation. The students begin their journey through the Gate of Humility; the original gate has since been moved to the Master's Garden, but the word 'Humilitatis' is inscribed next to the Porter's Lodge as a reminder. In the heart of the College is the Gate of Virtue; one of the first Renaissance style edifices in England. Finally, at Graduation, the students pass through the Gate of Honour: beyond its doors is the Senate House where the students are awarded their degrees. The six sundials on the gate's turret were refurbished in 1956 to commemorate the 400th anniversary of the College's refounding.

The College was originally founded as Gonville Hall in 1348 by Edmund Gonville, a parish priest from Norfolk. John Kees refounded the College in 1557 after it had fallen into a state of disrepair. Having attended the Hall as an undergraduate and Fellow of humanities he later became interested in medicine and travelled to Padua to study the discipline. During his stay he was influenced by the Italian Renaissance whose architecture later inspired the designs for the three gates and Caius Court.

Of the many students to walk through the College gates, a number have excelled to become the leading authorities in their field. Dr. Cauis himself introduced the study of practical anatomy to England, and William Harvey discovered the circulation of blood. A more recent Fellow is Professor Stephen Hawking, the Lucasian Professor of Mathematics and author of *A Brief History of Time*. The College has hosted five Nobel Prize winners. These include Francis Crick who unravelled DNA during his time as a Fellow in the 1960's and James Chadwick who earned his prize by discovering the neutron.

Above: *Gate of Honour*
Top left: *Gargoyle*

CORPUS CHRISTI

Corpus Christi is unique. It is the only Cambridge or Oxford college founded by townspeople. Two Cambridge Guilds, the Guild of Corpus Christi and the Guild of St. Mary, united and obtained royal license in 1352 to found the College. Although the Guilds were commercial establishments, they existed primarily for religious and charitable purposes. The College was founded in an effort to heal the old feuds between the town and University, and to replace the clergy who had died during the Black Death. It was written in the statutes that the chaplains and scholars must pray for the souls of the fraternity members forever.

The dark, low houses and crooked roofs of Old Court make up the oldest surviving college court in Cambridge. This medieval court, built in 1370, was the first closed quadrangle court, designed to provide a private and peaceful environment for study, and to protect its scholars from the town. Despite being founded by the townspeople, the College bore the brunt of their displeasure when the Peasants Revolt arrived in Cambridge in 1381 - the Gates and buildings were set alight and much of the College was damaged.

Nevertheless, the ingenuity of the Fellows throughout the years has ensured that the College retains two impressive collections. Their pre-Reformation collection of silver is the finest in the country. During the Civil War, rather than give their plate and wealth to the King or the Parliamentarians, the College distributed the collection among the Fellows, giving them 'general leave of absence'. A drinking horn, older that the College itself, is still passed around and sipped from at Commemoration Feasts.

The Corpus Christi library holds some of the most important manuscripts in English history. The collection owes much to Matthew Parker, Master between 1544-53, who saved many works from destruction after the dissolution of the monasteries. He was appointed Archbishop of Canterbury by Elizabeth I, and as only the second protestant Archbishop he collected thousands of manuscripts to support arguments for the basis of the new Church of England, and to translate the Bible from Latin to English.

LEFT: *Corpus Chapel. Before it was built the scholars, having no chapel of their own, worshipped in the nearby church of St. Bene't's. Their ties to the church were so strong that until the 1820s, the College was popularly known as Bene't College.*

MAGDALENE

Magdalene is a college divided into two halves by a busy road. Its main gates lead precariously onto Magdalene Street, formerly a slum lined with brothels just outside the city boundaries. Behind the west gate, a path meanders through open courts with a village feel to them, and the lawns lead down to the river where the Magdalene punts are moored. The river Cam flows under Magdalene Bridge and along the length of the College. Through the east gate are the main courts, the Hall - still lit only by candlelight, and the Pepys Building.

Samuel Pepys was an undergraduate at Magdalene and throughout his career as a Member of Parliament, Secretary to the Admiralty and President of the Royal Society, he kept diaries in which he also recounted his return visits to the College. He particularly remembered the fine beer he drank 'I took my boy… and there drank my belly full of their beer, which pleased me, as the best I ever drank…'

Pepys bequeathed his library of 3000 books, including the six volumes of his diaries written in shorthand, first to his nephew and then in 1724 to Magdalene 'entire in one body… for the benefit of posterity'. No books were to be added or removed. The collection is catalogued by size, the smaller books raised on book-shaped blocks so that they remain level.

Behind the Library lie the Fellows' Gardens. Fine lawns lead down through the trees to the river's edge. Another path takes the visitor through a small wood, past the Victorian Pet Cemetery where the Masters traditionally bury their cats and dogs, and on up the bank to the low wall which secludes the gardens from the busy road behind.

*The Victorian Pet Cemetery where over the centuries
the Masters have buried their cats and small dogs.*

Benson's Court

Bright's Building, Quayside

The Chapel contains the Adoration of the Magi painted by Rubens in eight days in 1634. It was given to King's College in 1961 and now stands above the altar, the floor of which had to be lowered in order to accommodate the painting.

KING'S

Founded in 1446 exclusively for boys from Eton, King's College began with a strict set of statutes decreeing that members should not wear long hair, beards or coloured shoes. Until 1859, it was the duty of the college Porters to shave any unruly student who passed through the gates. The young Etonians were however, granted special privileges; they did not sit examinations for their degrees nor answer to the authority of the University's Proctors. Tensions arose when other colleges became jealous of such privileges. In 1454, they attacked King's College with 'guns and habiliments of war'.

Through the centuries King's College has developed a reputation for tolerance and progressive thinking. During times of religious change in the 16th century, the College removed the high altar after the Reformation, restored it under the catholic rule of Mary Tudor, modified it during the reign of protestant Elizabeth I and removed it again under the puritan Oliver Cromwell. Similarly the sermons delivered in King's Chapel by Benjamin Whichcote in the 17th century were a model of moderate thinking in the Church; he expressed the radical belief that individuals' opinions should be tolerated. In modern times the College's progressive policies linger; it was the first to dispose of compulsory gown-wearing, to introduce female students and is one of the leading colleges in the effort to balance the ratio of private to state school entrants.

Its tolerance extends to the statue of Henry VI on Provost Lodge occasionally being seen dressed up in a flat cap and college scarf on cold days, and given a pumpkin on Halloween nights. Students have also added washing up liquid to the fountain to watch the bubbles float across the courts. The chapel spires have also become a centre of attention as dangerous attempts have been made to conquer them. In 1965, conscientious climbers hung a large 'Peace in Vietnam' banner between two of the spires.

The King's Screen (above) was designed and built in the early 19th century by the architect William Wilkins. As an undergraduate at Cambridge he won a scholarship to travel and study classical Greek and Roman architecture, whose influence can be noted in his work on Downing College and London's National Gallery. His neo-gothic design for the King's Screen, which echoes certain features of the Chapel, is often mistaken for a medieval work, demonstrating his mastery of many different styles.

TOP LEFT: *King's College Chapel*
LEFT: *Gibb's Building*
ABOVE: *King's Screen*
TOP RIGHT: *King's Front Gate*

KING'S COLLEGE CHAPEL

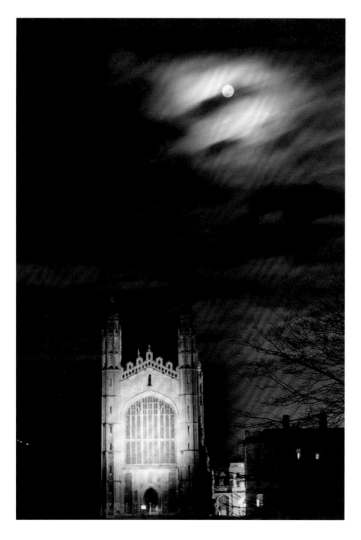

Truly a building of kings, it took four successive reigns to complete the Chapel. In 1446, Henry VI laid the first foundation stone, placing it where the high altar was to stand. When he was deposed during the Wars of the Roses in 1461, work stopped and only began again very slowly under Edward IV and Richard III. A different, buff coloured stone was used, clearly marking the stage of completion the chapel had reached under Henry VI. Encouraged by his mother, Lady Margaret of Beaufort, Henry VII completed the majority of the building and, when he died, Henry VIII provided for the Chapel's stained glass windows and wooden screen. The Chapel, 90 years in the making, was completed in 1536.

The different styles of each king are clearly visible. Henry VI aimed for the simple style found at the east end, while Henry VII chose a more ornate style placing Tudor roses and other royal emblems in prominent positions. With its fan vault ceiling and soaring spires, this is one of the finest Gothic buildings in all Europe.

LEFT: Every year on Christmas Eve, King's College Choir broadcasts the world famous 'Festival of Nine Lessons and Carols'. The performance always begins with a solo line of 'Once in Royal David's City' sung by one of the young choristers, who is only told he has been chosen for the honour a few moments before the concert.

QUEENS'

Queens' owes its existence to the Rector of St. Botolph's Church, Andrew Dockett, and to the generosity of two queens. Dockett founded St. Bernard's College in 1446 for one President and four Fellows, but in 1448, Margaret of Anjou obtained permission from her husband, Henry VI, to refound and rename it Queen's College, in emulation of his own King's College. Its third founding, by Elizabeth Woodville, Queen to Edward IV, saw the College move to a larger site and become Queens' College. It is now appropriately patronised by the Queen Mother to whom the Lyon court is dedicated, in honour of her maiden name.

Queens' boasts one of the two complete medieval courts in Cambridge (the other is at Corpus Christi). Once set amongst a vibrant part of the town in Milne Street, its intimate enclosed walls provided a welcome respite from the busy street. Inside, the walls are original examples of late-medieval brickwork, even showing the seams where building work stopped for winter in 1448. In First Court is the dial of 1733 which is both a sundial and a moondial, one of only a few in the world. The timber beams of the cloister court are a 15th century remnant and often photographed. They were fortunately preserved for centuries by plaster covering before being uncovered in 1911.

The wooden Mathematical Bridge has been the source of much speculation. Some claim it was built by mathematicians without using a single bolt, then ruined by engineers who dismantled it but were only able to rebuild it using bolts. In reality, this is no more than a myth; the bridge was indeed designed on mathematical principles in 1749 by William Etheridge, but built by James Essex using coach screws. The bridge that spans the Cam today is a 1905 replica held together with bolts.

Jesus Cockerel

JESUS

In 1496 John Alcock, Bishop of Ely, visited the 12th century nunnery of St. Radegund to find it had fallen into a state of decline. He found only two nuns in residence, one of whom was with child. Requesting a licence from King Henry VII, he suppressed the nunnery, and founded in its place 'The College of the Blessed Virgin Mary, St. John the Evangelist and the Glorious Virgin St. Radegund'. It is more commonly known as Jesus College, after the chapel of the former convent.

Alcock began by building a fine gate-tower at the end of the entrance path known as 'The Chimney', on which he placed his own statue and above it his rebus – a cockerel on a globe, an emblem repeated throughout the College. Situated above the kitchens is The Hall, originally the nuns' refectory, which has been used as a dining hall for over 800 years. The nuns' church became the College chapel, its tower is the oldest building in any of the Cambridge colleges. The burial ground of the nuns of St. Radegund still lies outside the east end of the Chapel. The intimate serenity of the Cloister Court, coupled with the open expanse of the larger courts and the College playing fields behind, conjure up images of the College's monastic beginnings.

Every two years the College holds an open-air exhibition of sculpture in its grounds. There are also a number of works on permanent loan, the most prominent of which is Barry Flanagan's horse, which stands in First Court and is a favourite amongst the students. The Porters discourage climbing onto it, but students still persist with their antics.

One of the College's more rebellious students was Samuel Taylor Coleridge, a famous poet and one of the founders of the Romantic movement. He matriculated at Jesus College in 1791, but later ran away to join the army because he owed the College so much money. Although he was asked to return, he still failed to complete his degree. The story goes that he and a friend were once found drunk in a gutter. When offered help he shouted "Save my friend, I can swim."

'The Chimney'

Jesus' Old Library houses a first edition copy of the first Bible printed in the New World. It was translated by the Jesus graduate John Eliot, and published in Cambridge, Massachusetts in 1663.

Archbishop Thomas Cranmer was an undergraduate and then a Fellow of Jesus College before becoming the first protestant Archbishop of Canterbury in 1533. He was largely responsible for the annulment of Henry VIII's marriage to Catherine of Aragon, and for the compilation of the Book of Common Prayer. When Mary Tudor came to the throne he was tried for high treason, then for heresy and in 1556 he was burnt at the stake in Oxford.

CHRIST'S

When originally founded as God's House in 1439 by William Byngham, the College focused its scholars on the lesser degree of Master of Grammar in order to replace the schoolmasters who had died during the Black Death. The Masters degree was split into the three-year Trivium of Grammar, Logic and Rhetoric, and the four-year Quadrivium of Music, Arithmetic, Geometry and Astronomy. Throughout the seven years they would also study the Three Philosophies – Moral, Metaphysical and Natural, and the two Learned Tongues – Greek and Hebrew. Students who successfully completed the seven years became Masters of Arts, which gave them the right to teach and ensured their future. Students now study a broad range of subjects and Christ's often heads the academic league tables.

God's House was refounded in 1505 by Lady Margaret Beaufort, Henry VII's mother, who renamed it Christ's College. Some of the buildings in First Court date from the days of God's House, but the majority of the Court and the Great Gate were built during Lady Margaret's lifetime.

The Fellows' Garden is extensive and features two of the College's highlights - the 18th century bathing pool and Milton's Mulberry Tree, allegedly one of the 300 mulberry trees bought by the College in 1608 to support James I's plans for an English silk trade. John Milton was a pale and delicate student who arrived at Christ's in 1625 and earned the nickname 'Lady of Christ's' which displeased him greatly. He reputedly wrote many of his early poems beneath the mulberry tree including *Ode on the Morning of Christ's Nativity*.

Another Christ's scholar was Charles Darwin, famous for his theory of evolution. Darwin matriculated at Christ's in 1828, agreeing to study for the Church as this would afford him the time to pursue his interests in natural sciences. While at Cambridge he befriended the Professor of Botany, John Henslow, who advised Darwin to join *HMS Beagle* on a voyage charting the continent of South America once he had completed his studies. On the five-year journey Darwin's study of the subtle differences in species throughout the continent led him to the theory that would change the commonly-held belief that God was the creator of species. Darwin's life-work study of nature culminated in the book *The Origin of Species*, first published in 1859.

ABOVE: *Fellow's Pool*
LEFT: *Christ's Second Court*

ST. JOHN'S

St. John's was built on the site of the 13th century Hospital of St. John, and, like Christ's, was founded by Lady Margaret Beaufort. Its seemingly endless sequence of courts are a splendour.

Building work on First Court began in 1511 and incorporated the Hospital chapel and infirmary whose foundation stone can still be seen on the lawn. The chapel that now completes the court was designed by George Gilbert Scott in 1834. The Gothic style commemorates its predecessor, the Hospital's 13th century chapel. The gatehouse is distinctly medieval, with its tall chimneys and heraldic carving. The court is surrounded by staircases leading up to students' and Fellows' rooms. Notably, on 'G' staircase, the words 'Stag. Nov 15, 1777' are carved into the lintel above the doorway to mark the incident when a stag was spied and killed in the staircase.

Second Court blends seamlessly into First court, although it was built 80 years later. Enclosed within its Elizabethan brickwork is one of Cambridge's most spectacular rooms, the panelled Senior Combination Room, formally called the Long Gallery (it is over 28 metres long). The plaster work on the ceiling dates from 1600 and the room is still lit by candlelight alone. During the Second World War the D-Day Landings were partly planned in this room. Today the room is used primarily as a common room for the Fellows.

The Bridge of Sighs' only resemblance to its Venetian namesake is that both are covered bridges. St. John's Bridge did not lead its students to torture or execution as its Venetian counterpart had done to the prisoners who crossed it.

RIGHT: *St. John's Gate*
TOP: *New Court Cloisters*
LEFT: *Bridge of Sighs*

Third Court houses the Old Library whose books are shelved on the upper storey, as was the custom, leaving the ground floor for other purposes. The 17th century style of this court offers a pleasant embellishment of the traditional red brickwork of the College. The chain of courts continues over the Bridge of Sighs which leads to New Court.

The magnificent neo-gothic New Court crowns the spectacular view from the open grounds on St. John's Backs. It was the largest single building of any college at the time of its completion in 1831. The battlements and turrets of the central tower have earned it the affectionate title of 'The Wedding Cake'.

The most modern building in the college, Cripp's Court, is greatly admired for its creation of modern and ordered yet romantic spaces. Constructed of Portland stone in 1967, it won the RIBA Bronze Medal architectural prize.

St. John's New Court

St. John's Chapel tower

37

TRINITY

Henry VIII's last major act was to found Trinity College in 1546: six weeks later he died. It is therefore largely due to a succession of energetic and magnanimous Masters that Trinity stands as Henry VIII had intended it to - as the largest and grandest of all the Cambridge colleges.

Originally on the site where Trinity now stands were two smaller, medieval colleges; King's Hall and Michealhouse. Henry VIII dissolved these two colleges, founded under Edward III, and built Trinity in their place. Great Gate is adorned with heraldry of Edward III and his sons, and the path between the Great Gate to the Master's Lodge was a medieval road that led to the gates of King's Hall.

Great Court was created some fifty years later in the 1600s by Dr. Thomas Nevile, the Master at the time. He was a wealthy man with strong views on architecture. In order to create the luxurious sense of space he demolished unwanted buildings and had the clock tower moved, stone-by-stone, 30 yards back to align with the Chapel. With two acres of lawns and pathways Great Court is the largest of the Oxbridge courts and known for The Great Court Run – an event immortalized in the film *Chariots of Fire* (filmed at Eton).

Every year, tradition states that as the clock strikes twelve, the Freshers must complete a lap of the Court before the final chime – the midnight run after Matriculation Dinner is not usually as successful as the midday run the following day.

Nevile's Court was begun under the same Master, Dr. Thomas Nevile, but he did not live to see its completion. The Wren library, designed by Sir Christopher Wren for no fee, completed the court in 1695. Wren deceives the onlooker by bringing the level of the Library floor down to the base of the arches, creating an extra half storey for the tall book shelves but maintaining the arcade line that runs round the court. The Wren Library holds a great number of medieval, rare and modern manuscripts ranging from the 8th century *Epistles of St. Paul*, to a manuscript from *Winnie the Pooh* by AA Milne; both AA Milne and his son Christopher Robin were students at Trinity College.

As an undergraduate at Trinity College, Lord Byron used to swim in the fountain by night and, as is it was forbidden to keep dogs, he kept a small bear in a corner tower of Great Court.

Trinity's academic achievements continued through the centuries and are now renowned the world over. The College claims more Nobel Prize Winners than France. The list of brilliant academics includes the like of Ramanujan, a mathematician whose manuscripts written in his village in India are still being translated; Edward Rutherford, for his work on the theory of the atom; and in 1998, Amartya Sen, for his redefinition of Third World economics.

In the ante chapel are the plaques of the Nobel Prize winners and statues of the famous Trinity men; among them Lord Tennyson, Francis Bacon and Sir Isaac Newton. As one of Trinity's most famous scholars, Newton is commemorated throughout the College; the statue in the ante chapel, a stained glass window and his notebook and library of books in the Wren Library. His manuscripts are kept in the University Library. There is an impressive echo beneath the Library and around the court; between these arches Newton took his first rough measurement of the speed of sound, by tapping his foot, watching a clock, and recording the length of time before the echo was heard. The small apple tree planted to the right of Great Gate is reputedly a descendent of the tree from which an apple fell onto the physicist's head.

EMMANUEL

Male Mandarin duck

Emmanuel is home to a variety of species of exotic and indigenous ducks from Mandarins and Carolinas to Mallards. Ducks, unlike the students, are allowed to walk on the grass in Front Court.

'The Jester' by Anne Taylor

Emmanuel College stands on land that was once a Dominican Friary, destroyed during the Reformation in 1537. It was founded in 1584 by Walter Mildmay, Chancellor of the Exchequer to Elizabeth I. The College was at the forefront of the Puritan movement: when the Puritans emigrated to America in the 1630s for fear of persecution, so many were from Emmanuel that New England was referred to as 'Emmanuel's Land'. John Harvard is the most renowned of the many Puritans from Emmanuel to voyage to America. When he died in New Town (now Cambridge, Mass.) he left his library of 320 books and half his estate to found a new school, now Harvard University. Emmanuel's 'Brick Building', built in the 1630s still hosts a Harvard Scholar every year.

Emmanuel boasts one of three Cambridge buildings designed by Sir Christopher Wren. The Wren Chapel replaced one used by the Puritans, formerly a Dominican refectory which was 'incorrectly' aligned North to South. Wren's East to West Chapel, Baroque in influence, conceals a gallery which runs the full length of its thirteen windows. It was used 'for exercise in bad weather' and is now a fine reception room. At the time, Wren's Chapel was the fourth side of a court of Tudor buildings. Now little of the original buildings remain, having been replaced by more neo-classical style buildings in the 18th century. The dining hall, built on the site of the old monastery, was designed by James Essex, who also built the College's neo-classical front entrance.

The Queen's Building is Emmanuel's newest architectural addition. Designed by Sir Michael and Lady Hopkins and funded by College benefactors, it is built of the same pinkish Ketton stone used for the Wren Chapel, and contains a soundproof auditorium and a number of common rooms.

One of Emmanuel's architectural advantages is its low walls. During the 11pm curfews of the 1950s and 60s, the students could jump back into the College if they were caught outside after the gates were locked. At the same time if a visiting women were caught inside they incurred a severe penalty. When in 1979 women were first invited to study at Emmanuel, all the wide beds were replaced by thinner ones.

The paddock in summer is a scene of students relaxing and playing tennis amidst colourful flora and fauna. Its lake, once fished in by Dominican Friars, is home to many exotic and local ducks – one of Emmanuel's most endearing traits. 'The Jester' is a sculpture of great intrigue and the weeping Oriental Plane tree in the Fellows' Garden is nearly 200 years old. The lines painted along the bottom of the 300-year-old swimming pool served to guide Fellows who swam beneath the surface through the algae. Now of course the pool is cleaned.

SIDNEY SUSSEX

The site on which Sidney Sussex stands was formerly a Franciscan friary, demolished during the Reformation and thereafter dismantled to provide stone for Trinity College. Members of Trinity College were reluctant to sell the land to the executors of the founder, Lady Frances Sidney, and only conceded when they received a strongly worded letter from Queen Elizabeth I, who then granted Sidney Sussex its charter. The Elizabethan buildings have been rebuilt and remodeled, particularly during the 19th century. Battlements, gables and Roman cement covering the red brick buildings all contribute to the Gothic theme.

Oliver Cromwell studied at Sidney Sussex from 1616. When Cromwell went on to become Cambridge's Member of Parliament and Lord Protector of England, Sidney Sussex was mostly spared the hardships of the Civil War due to its Puritan background. The colleges, which for the most part supported the king, were taken over by Puritan authorities in the region. Many lost their valuable collections of plate in loans to help fund the king. Chapels and churches were destroyed to remove idolatry, college Masters were replaced, and buildings were used as garrisons for the army. Sidney Sussex was mostly unharmed, unlike many of the colleges.

Cromwell's head now lies buried in the ante chapel, its journey there mysterious and undoubtedly extraordinary; it was presented to the College in 1960.

DOWNING

Built on a field used for shooting fowl, Downing College is a vast, open college hidden behind Regent Street. The understated gate gives no indication of the spacious grounds or the impressive neo-classical buildings beyond it. King George III recommended that the College devote itself to the classical style, and the chosen architect, William Wilkins, was pleased to oblige. He had travelled to Greece and Rome to study classical architecture and his designs for a three-sided court open to the south, with its trees and orderly paths, are often said to have pre-empted the American style campus.

Downing was only founded after a succession of deaths, family feuds and many years of legal battles. The endowment for the College was left by Sir George Downing; grandson of the creator of Downing Street in London. By 1800, when the courts finally found in favour of Sir George's will, the funds were substantially depleted. In order to finance the building work, the College sold half its land which was developed into the Downing Site where there are a number of important University museums and laboratories.

Each new building follows the original plan drawn up by Wilkins, providing a new interpretation of the neo-classical style every time.

ABOVE: Master's Lodge
RIGHT: Library

*There are no 'Please Keep Off The Grass' signs at Newnham
College, but for many years there were a strict set of rules to obey.
Newnham's first Principal, Miss Clough, ensured that 'her girls'
were chaperoned at all times, that they did not cycle in shopping
streets, nor smoke, nor partake in amateur dramatic groups.*

NEWNHAM

Newnham College was the second women's college to be built, and
unlike its predecessor, Girton College, Newnham remains a women-
only college. It was brought into being in 1875 by Henry Sidgwick, a
Fellow of Trinity and one of Cambridge's leading supporters of women's
education, but was not officially founded or granted college status until
some fifty years later. Women were allowed to sit the University Tripos
Exams from 1881, but were not awarded degrees for their efforts until
1921, and were not official members of the University until 1948.

Henry Sidgwick and his advisors were careful to provide a suitable
environment for women. The picturesque site with its warm red brick,
sizeable bay windows and brilliant white woodwork all contribute to
the homely feel of the College. There are no courts for two reasons; the
stairwells leading off the courts caused upward drafts, and, were the
College to fail, the large buildings with rooms branching off from long
corridors would have sold more easily.

The College flourished. It produced many eminent women, among
them the poet Sylvia Plath, the actress Emma Thompson, and the
brilliant mathematician Philippa Fawcett.

Newnham Old Hall

THE UNIVERSITY

The University had a humble beginning when, in 1209, a group of students and teachers arrived in Cambridge from Oxford. By 1226, the University had appointed a Chancellor and Regent Masters to govern the students, and the organisation of the emerging institution began to take shape. The University received official recognition in 1318 when Pope John XXII licensed it as a 'Studium Generale'.

The colleges were and continue to be founded as independent, self-governing bodies. In recent times, many new colleges such as Churchill, Robinson, and Newhall have been built, and other institutions such as Fitzwilliam and Hughes Hall have been converted to colleges and given University status. Students apply to a college, which then admits them to the University. The college still provides the student with accommodation and food, and although the private 'supervisions' (small group tutorials) are still given by the Fellows in college, lectures and research now take place in one of the University's many departments.

The research carried out in these departments over the years has had an enormous influence on the understanding of the world in which we live. To name but a few of the great minds – from 1760, Henry Cavendish studied hydrogen gas and later ascertained that the union of hydrogen and oxygen resulted in water. In the 19th century, Charles Babbage defined the operation of a computer long before it was known how to build one. Alan Turing, the brilliant mathematician, deciphered the codes transmitted from the German Enigma machines during the Second World War. Paul Dirac, one of the founders of Quantum Physics, held the Lucasian Professorship of Mathematics for 40 years in the 20th century, a position once held by Isaac Newton, and now held by Professor Stephen Hawking. Cambridge University's list of academic dignitaries and Nobel Laureates is nothing short of astounding.

The front door

In medicine, the Addenbrookes Hospital in Cambridge is one of the world's leading research hospitals. Between 1961 and 1984, the hospital was moved due to shortage of space from its building on Trumpington Street to a larger site on the outskirts of town. In 1995, the former Addenbrookes building was converted into a colourful new University department; the Institute of Management Studies.

Through the University's science and engineering departments, business in Cambridge has developed at a phenomenal rate since the 1960s. The University began to allow its researchers to own their intellectual property and encouraged the development of commercial enterprises. The Science Park and St. John's Innovation Centre were developed on the outskirts of Cambridge to house these technology start-ups. Now Cambridge is home to hundreds of technology start-ups and a number of billion-pound companies. A town once thought of as a rural backwater is now referred to as Silicon Fen.

Judge Institute of Management Studies, formerly Addenbrookes Hospital

THE BOAT RACE CAMBRIDGE VS OXFORD

The internationally famous Boat Race, which attracts millions of viewers worldwide every year, began as a challenge between friends in 1829. Charles Merivel from Cambridge and Charles Wordsworth of Oxford organised the first boat race at Henley-upon-Thames. It was such a resounding success that the townspeople of Henley decided to organise their own regatta - now the Henley Royal Regatta. Every year the loser of the previous race challenges the winner to a new race. Early races were held at Westminster, but as crowds became too large, it was moved to the quiet village of Putney in 1845. The gruelling four and a half mile course from Putney to Mortlake has been raced annually ever since.

THE BUMPS

The Bumping of boats is a rowing event which attracts up to 2000 rowers twice a year; in Lent term and in May. The townspeoples' Bumps are held in the summer. Invented because the Cam is not wide enough to race the boats side by side, the crews are made to chase one another with the aim of 'bumping' the boat ahead. At the start, 15 boats are staggered along the river, separated by just a boat-and-a-half's length. The gun fires and pandemonium ensues as each boat races to catch the boat ahead. Boats that 'bump' move up in the starting order the next day, swapping places with the boat they bumped. A crew that successfully bumps on all four days of the event is awarded 'blades' - a rowing blade enscribed with the names of the crew and date of their victory. The overall winners become 'Head of the River', and traditionally burn a boat at Bumps Dinner to celebrate.

ABOVE: *Cambridge Blues - 1997 Boat Race*
RIGHT: *Bumps - one minute after the gun*
Photos courtesy of J.E.T. Photographic

MAY BALLS

The May Balls take place during May Week, which is in June. Students celebrate the end of their exams with a week of garden parties, plays, concerts and May Balls, all of which are arranged by different societies and colleges. The May Balls are a lavish affair with food and drink all night, music and dancing, and sometimes fairgrounds, casinos, comedy tents and ballroom dancing. The tradition of the Cambridge May Balls began in 1866 when Trinity First and Third Boat Club decided to celebrate their success on the river that year. They held the first May Ball in the local Lion Hotel, attended by 300 people. It was a great success and became an annual event, later moving to the College grounds. Many colleges have since followed suit; there is at least one May Ball every night of May Week.

Trinity May Ball: the survivors, 6 am.
Photo courtesy of J.E.T. Photographic

THE CONGREGATIONS

The University holds ten Congregations during the year, at which graduands are awarded their degrees and become graduates. The majority of the undergraduates proceed to their degree over the course of three days in late June. The rules for the graduation ceremonies at Cambridge are strictly enforced and remain traditional. Each of the colleges - beginning with King's, Trinity and St. John's, then in order of founding - hold their own procession from the college to the Senate House. The graduands wear long college gowns and a coloured hood; the colour indicating the degree they read. They process to the Senate House in order of precedence beginning with the Masters of Divinity, Law, Engineering and Natural Sciences. These are followed by the Bachelors of Veterinary Medicine, Music, Arts, Education and Theology. Once inside the Senate House, the graduands are presented to their Master, four at a time, by the Praelector. They must each hold a finger while he recites the Latin words that admit them to their degree, then kneel individually before their Master, place their hands in his and bow their heads as he in turn grants them their degree. The graduate stands and is handed his degree certificate on his way out to the green where the new graduates meet with their families and friends.

SILVER STREET

Detail of a charter which, in 1575, granted Cambridge a Coat of Arms. Charters were documents drawn up by the courts in response to requests or complaints made to the Crown by its subjects. These documents are now important historical records.Cambridge's oldest surviving charter was granted by King John in 1201, and a 1951 charter, issued by King George VI, awards Cambridge its city status.

ABOUT TOWN

Although often overshadowed by the University, the town has always played an important role in its own right. Cambridge was a busy market town for centuries before the arrival of the University.

Merchants' houses lined the streets from the town centre to the wharves by the river. The School of Pythagoras, a 12th century merchant's house fancifully named on the grounds that Pythagoras taught there, still stands in the grounds of St. John's College. Over the centuries, much of the town was taken over by the colleges. The important land that led from the river to the town's high street was flattened for the expansion of King's College in the 1450s, but the plans were halted and the land lay bare for 300 years. This was a source of much friction between Town and Gown, and the townspeople often expressed their displeasure at the power of the University which was favoured by the Monarchy. During the Civil War, the town supported Oliver Cromwell and the Parliamentarians while the University members were Royalists.

As well as trading at the market, Cambridge was granted charters by the king to hold four fairs each year on the fields that surrounded the town. Midsummer Fair, so named because it was traditionally held on Midsummer's Day, was first recorded in 1103 in the Barnwell Parish archives, and is still held every year on Midsummer Common. Stourbridge Fair was one of the largest trading fairs in Europe. Traders came in to Cambridge by boat, travelling up the Great Ouse and the river Cam, and coaches brought visitors from London. Defoe described the Stourbridge Fair in 1722 in his book *A tour through the whole island of Great Britain* as 'not only the greatest in the whole nation, but in the whole world'. It ran for up to five weeks every year from medieval times to the early 20th century.

ABOVE: *12th century merchant's house - now named 'The School of Pythagoras'*
TOP LEFT: *1575 charter granting Cambridge its Coat of Arms (photograph by Phillip Mynott)*

THE ROUND CHURCH

The Church of the Holy Sepulchre, commonly known as The Round Church, is one of only four round churches in England. It was originally built in 1130 when the Crusaders returned from Jerusalem where they had seen the round church on the traditional site where Jesus is said to have risen from the dead. They built a circular nave and a small chancel; the polygonal belfry and the larger windows were added in the 15th century. The Victorian congregations, displeased with the previous alterations, had the church extensively restored in 1841. They replaced the bell tower with a conical roof and reverted to pseudo-Norman windows. They enlarged the chancel, built a new south aisle and cleaned all the stonework. During the Second World War, a bomb fell just twenty yards from the church, despite an agreement that no party would bomb Oxford, Cambridge or Heidelberg. Fortunately, only the stained glass window on the east side was damaged. Tired of death and destruction, the townspeople chose to portray the Crucifixion as a scene of life and continuance. Christ's eyes are wide open, and his cross is the Tree of Life.

ST. BOTOLPH'S

St. Botolph was an abbot in East Anglia during the 7th century and, like St. Christopher, was made a patron saint of travellers. Churches dedicated to St. Botolph are often found near the gates of a city. The one in Cambridge was built just inside the town's medieval Trumpington Gate, near the main road to London. Travellers prayed for a good journey before setting off, and gave thanks in the church when they arrived. 'Botolph's Town' in Lincolnshire became Boston, which later gave its name to Boston in Massachusetts.

ST. BENE'T'S

St. Bene't's is the oldest church in Cambridge; the tower and parts of the nave date from the founding of the church in 1025. The six bells were possibly the first in the country to ring an organised peal (when the bells are rung in formation) as the inventor of change ringing, Fabian Stedman, was parish clerk at St. Bene't's in the 1670s.

ST. MARY THE GREAT

For centuries St. Mary the Great has been the principal church in Cambridge. It serves both the University and the city, and consequently holds the unique position of performing both spiritual and civic duties. The University held lectures and degree ceremonies in the church, and kept the University Chest there which was broken open and plundered during the Peasants Revolt in 1381. University Sermons are still preached in St. Mary the Great, and the Mayor and Corporation of the City of Cambridge hold important civic events there. The galleries inside were added in 1735 as the University grew. They were designed by James Gibb, who also designed the Senate House opposite, and included a raised platform at the east end where the Proctors sat, keeping a watchful eye over students during the Sermons.

Many of the Reformation leaders preached at St. Mary the Great; a brass plate near the altar shows where the German Lutheran Martin Bucer was buried in 1552. His coffin was later exhumed during Mary Tudor's reign and burnt in the market place, but soil from the site was placed in a coffin and was re-buried in the church during Elizabeth I's reign.

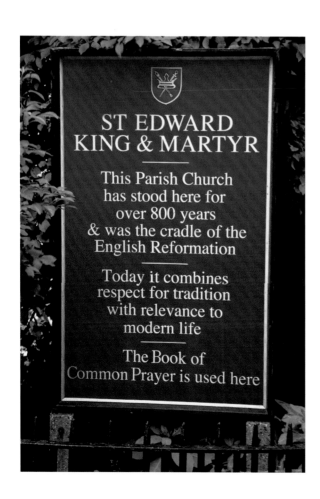

St. Bene't's Tower

ST. EDWARD KING AND MARTYR

St. Edward King and Martyr was dedicated to the Saxon King Edward the Martyr, murdered by his stepmother in 978. Today the church is better known for its close associations with the early Reformers and is referred to as 'The Cradle of the English Reformation'. It was in this church, tucked away in a little square behind King's Parade, that the leaders of the movement preached the new doctrines. A plaque at the door commemorates the martyrs Thomas Bilney of Trinity Hall, one of the first leaders; Robert Barnes, Prior of the Augustinian monastery; and Hugh Latimer, a Fellow of Clare College and a gifted preacher who was burnt at the stake during the reign of Mary Tudor. Inside, the 16th century oak pulpit from which Latimer preached is still in its place by the altar.

Market from Great St. Mary's Tower

MARKET

The market place has been the bustling heart of the city since medieval times. It was formerly an L-shape that ran from Market Hill, around a group of houses that stood on what is now the market square, and on round to the north end of Peas Hill - so called because the fish market, 'piscaria' in Latin, was held there. The market was divided into sections; corn and poultry were sold at the north-east end, while butter and milk were sold further down alongside the Garden Market. The fish market came next, followed by the Beast Market, which was not far from where the Corn Exchange now stands.

The present day market came into existence when, in 1849, the Great Fire of Cambridge destroyed many of the houses and shops on Market Hill. Plans were drawn up to re-design the market place, and by 1855, the town had an open, rectangular market place with an elaborate fountain. Today the market is a colourful spectacle of local produce from fruit and vegetables, fresh fish and cheese to new and second hand clothes, books, music and souvenirs.

Hobson's Conduit, now on Trumpington Road, was originally part of the market place. It was moved to its present site after the Great Fire in 1849 when its limited supply of water could not quench the fire in time and the market place had to be re-designed.

PORTUGAL PLACE

Portugal Place is a secluded haven of Georgian town houses with little steps that lead up to low front doors. Large paving stones slant down towards the narrow drain that runs along the middle of the quiet pedestrian way towards Jesus Green at the lower end of the street.

The top of Portugal Place near St. Clement's church was originally called Clement's Passage. The name changed when builders found Portuguese coins on the site where more houses were built in the mid 19th century. From the 18th century, port, the sweet fortified Portuguese wine, was a key import delivered at Quayside, not far from Portugal Place. At the time, relations with France were poor and port was favoured against French wine.

Today the houses in Portugal Place are privately owned by some of the colleges and individual families. The Nobel Prize winner Francis Crick and his wife lived at No. 20, and in the early 1900s the Pakistani philosopher, Muhammad Iqbal, lodged at No. 17 for a year while studying at Trinity College.

EDE AND RAVENSCROFT

Ede and Ravenscroft have been making ceremonial robes for over 300 years and are the appointed robemakers to the Queen and HRH Prince of Wales. The Shudall family founded the firm in London in 1689, tailoring robes for the State, Church and Law. Today they own shops in London, Cambridge, Oxford, Edinburgh and St. Petersburg, producing robes for everyone from University graduands to Knights of the Garter.

HOBSON'S CONDUIT

Hobson's Conduit was built in 1610 to improve sanitation - it provided Cambridge with fresh drinking water for 250 years. The conduit brought water from the springs south of Cambridge to the heart of the town and the market place. The water flowed along runnels (narrow stone gullies between the pavement and the road) on St. Andrew's Street and Trumpington Street; those in Trumpington Street are still present. The conduit was named after the entrepreneurial Thomas Hobson. He owned a coaching inn and loaned horses, but would only offer his clients the horse which had rested longest, hence the phrase 'Hobson's Choice', meaning no choice at all.

THE PICKEREL

The Pickerel claims to be the oldest pub in Cambridge. During the 16th century it was one of five inns along Magdalene Street; the well-endowed gargoyles opposite the College are remnants of the Cross Keys Inn which, like many inns, was also a brothel. The Pickerel was the only inn to survive and photographs inside suggest that little of the façade has changed over the years, although the inn was once a much larger establishment, with its own brewery. Photographs also show the pub's close affiliation with Magdalene College; the football teams and rowing eights adorn the walls in their full glory. The Pickerel was frequented by Samuel Pepys and by C. S. Lewis during their years as undergraduates at the College and is still very popular with the Magdalene students.

THE EAGLE

The Eagle is steeped in history. It began as a coaching inn and post house during the 17th century; the charming courtyard with its hanging flower baskets was once the site of the inn's stables. The back room, known as the 'RAF Bar', is where the RAF and USAF airmen from the region's military bases signed their names on the ceiling with candle smoke during the Second World War. The pub was also a favourite watering hole of Crick and Watson in the early 1950s during their pioneering research into DNA. Their laboratories were across the road at the Downing Site, and they frequently came to The Eagle to rest and discuss their ideas.

THE GREEN DRAGON

The Green Dragon was granted its licence in 1630, making it the second oldest pub in Cambridge. During the Civil War, Cromwell stayed at the inn located by the river while his men kept watch on the banks. The bridge opposite has replaced the punt ferries that were used to cross the river *en route* from Cambridge to the medieval village of Chesterton. The pub's interior is traditional in style, with low ceilings, wooden beams and a stone fireplace.

FREE PRESS

The Free Press began life as a printing house, although it only printed one issue of its free paper before becoming a pub. Inside is a cosy space hidden at the back with its own bar known as The Snug. It once had its own entrance which local builders used to avoid traipsing cement through the rest of the pub. A record 61 people have fitted into the 10ft by 4ft space. Customers are fined for smoking or using mobile phones, and music and fruit machines are banned. Former owners ran the famous Free Press Boat Club, now renamed the Cambridge Blue after their new pub on Gwydir Street, an establishment that serves many fine English ales.

FITZWILLIAM MUSEUM

The Fitzwilliam Museum is a magnificent sight both inside and out. It was founded in 1816 when the 7th Viscount Fitzwilliam of Merrion bequeathed his collection of paintings, books, manuscripts and prints to his former University 'for the purpose of promoting the increase of learning and the other great objects of that noble Foundation'. This generous donation encouraged others to follow suit, and very soon the Fitzwilliam was exhibiting works from contemporary European paintings to Egyptian antiquities. The Museum's most influential director was S.C. Cockerell (1908 - 1937). 'I found it a pig stye, I turned it into a palace'. He not only transformed the Museum, he also revolutionized the way pictures were exhibited. Rather than hang them over the entire wall from ceiling to floor, he arranged them in a single or double line, a style now taken for granted.

The Fitzwilliam Museum is one of the oldest public museums in the country and was the first to hold a national collection of paintings.

Top: *Fitzwilliam Lion*
Above: *Fitzwilliam Museum*

CAMBRIDGE & COUNTY FOLK MUSEUM

The Folk Museum is a charming labyrinth of little rooms with low ceilings, creaky wooden floorboards and spiralling staircases. Each room houses a large array of personal and household objects as well as tools, clothes and toys used by the local people of Cambridge over the last 300 years. The children's nursery is full of traditional, brightly coloured toys and dolls' houses. The timber framed house is one of Cambridge's oldest dwelling houses. It became the White Horse Inn during the 17th century; the old hearth and bottle bar remain and are displayed upstairs.

According to English folklore, a child's shoe placed deep in the home wall wards off evil spirits, and if placed in a well, ensures the well will never run dry.

TOP: *Free School Lane signpost*
ABOVE: *Folk Museum*

KETTLE'S YARD

As guests at Kettle's Yard, the former home of Jim and Helen Ede, visitors are invited to enjoy the Edes' philosophy that art is a part of everyday living and should be enjoyed in the home alongside natural and household objects. The light and airy cottage with its wooden floorboards, low ceilings and open-plan rooms is a haven of peace and tranquillity in the busy city centre. Jim and Helen lived there for sixteen years, befriending and encouraging aspiring young artists and helping them financially by purchasing their works. In 1966 they donated the house, furniture and their collection to Cambridge University so that visitors would continue to enjoy the art they had collected over the years in the atmospheric house. The University added the large extension in 1970, where the charm of the cottage with its simple furniture and beautiful objects was continued in the new rooms. Kettle's Yard Gallery was also built at this time, adjacent to the house, to accommodate more contemporary art exhibitions.

ABOVE: *The Gallery at Kettle's Yard*

SCOTT POLAR RESEARCH INSTITUTE

The Scott Polar Research Institute has become one of the world's most important archives for Arctic and Antarctic data and research. Corridors of books, manuscripts and maps hold the secrets of the ice caps, their geology and ecosystems. The trials and hardships endured by Scott, Shackleton and their men during their expedition to the South Pole and back are clear for all to see in the small, evocative museum. The equipment they trusted their lives with is strikingly rudimentary, and the diaries and photographs on display relate their obvious courage and comradeship.

WHIPPLE MUSEUM OF THE HISTORY OF SCIENCE

The Whipple Museum displays a vast collection of scientific instruments and models. Nearly 2000 antique books and instruments, from microscopes and telescopes to sundials and early slide rules, were donated in 1944 to the University by Robert S. Whipple, Director of Cambridge Scientific Instrument Company. Many of the instruments, beautifully ornate and still in working order, were used by the University and the colleges from as early as the 16th century. On the right is a 1715 Ptolemaic; an instrument describing the sun's orbit around the earth!

TOP RIGHT: *Scott Polar Museum*
CENTRE: *Universal Equinoctial Sundial (photo courtesy of Whipple Museum)*
LOWER RIGHT: *Ptolemaic (photo courtesy of Whipple Museum)*

BOTANIC GARDEN

The Botanic Garden exhibits over 10,000 different species of plants and trees. They have been collected from all over the world for research purposes and creatively landscaped into different settings, such as pine forests, fenlands and tropical gardens. Cambridge's Professor of Botany, John Henslow, best known for inspiring the young Charles Darwin, recognised the need to study plants in an open, living habitat to discover how they survive and evolve. Consequently in 1846, he founded the Botanic Garden, replacing a smaller plot of 5 acres with 40 acres of garden large enough to accommodate families of trees, particularly those being discovered at the time in North America and Eastern Asia.

The long avenue leading to the fountain includes some of Britain's oldest giant redwoods and the first trees of the Dawn Redwood variety to be grown outside their native China. Alpine plants from mountains of every continent climb the rock garden, and narrow paths wind their way through the different flower beds and exhibits where every species is clearly labelled with its Latin name. In the glass house are some 3000 species ranging from palms and tropical plants to desert cacti. Air plants and orchids hang down from their trees, surviving on nutrients from the air, light and moisture in the warm environment.

ABOVE: *Glass house*
TOP RIGHT: *Lake and rock garden*
RIGHT: *Fountain*

PUNTING

Punting is one of Cambridge's long-standing traditions. The idyllic summer punting experience requires a lazy summer's day, with champagne, strawberries, a picnic and several long hours to spare. The flat-bottomed, shallow wooden boats were originally used to transport goods and livestock, often cattle, along the river Cam, and to hunt duck on the waterlogged Fens. Today punts are used for pleasure, and occasionally for racing. In Cambridge the punter stands at the rear of the boat; the pole is flung down into the water, leant back upon and then twisted to release it from the mud. The punter then uses it to manoeuvre the boat, negotiating his way between the many other punts, bridges and weeping willow branches. On a hot summer's day this is thirsty work, and not an easy technique to grasp; many a novice has fallen overboard, lost his pole in the mud or found himself suspended above the water, clinging to his pole while the punt glides gently away.

THIS PAGE: *Scudamore's Boat Yard*
RIGHT: *St. John's Backs*

Professional punters, the punt chauffeurs, recount the history and tales of the colleges and sites *en route* between Quayside and The Mill Pool. Aside from their historical and architectural knowledge, the chauffeurs are well known for entertaining embellishments and dubious facts; according to some chauffeurs, Silver Street holds the loot from the Great Train Robbery, and the large, old tree in St. John's Fellows' Gardens was planted by Jesus Christ when he visited Cambridge over 2000 years ago…

Some of the amazing stories are true. In 1956, a group of undergraduates punted a small car up the Cam to the Bridge of Sighs and suspended it from the Bridge with its wheels skimming the surface of the water.

ABOVE: *Punt chauffeur*
LEFT: *Trinity punts*
PREVIOUS PAGE: *The Bridge of Sighs*

Grey Sqirrel - Jesus Green

Canada Goose - The Backs

Mallards - Churchill College

Narcissus & Chinodoxia - Clare Fellows' Garden

Tulips - Trinity Avenue

Crocus and Snowdrops - Christ's College

Rudbeckia - Clare Fellows' Garden

GRANTCHESTER

'...oh! Yet
Stands the clock at ten to three?
And is there honey still for tea?'

The Old Vicarage, Grantchester.
Rupert Brooke 1912

Just two miles up stream from Cambridge lies Grantchester; a little English village with thatched cottages and country pubs made famous by Rupert Brooke's poem 'The Old Vicarage, Grantchester'. Many still punt up the Cam or walk through Grantchester Meadows to the village where, as a young graduate of King's in 1909, Brooke took rooms, first at Orchard House and later at The Old Vicarage. He was frequently visited by some of the great names of the age, friends who attended the University with him; the writers E.M. Forster and Virginia Woolf, the economist Maynard Keynes and the philosophers Bertrand Russell and Ludwig Wittgenstein. They spent much of their time at The Orchard - a tea garden in an apple orchard dating back to 1868, where traditional English tea with scones, jam, honey and cake is still served today. For seventy years it has been a tradition to punt to The Orchard for breakfast after May Balls.

TOP: *'The Local'*
TOP RIGHT: *Grantchester Meadows*
RIGHT: *Tea at the Orchard*

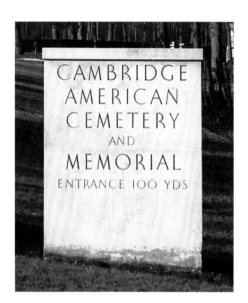

AMERICAN MILITARY CEMETERY

This monument is dedicated to the soldiers, sailors, airmen and coastguards who gave their lives during the Second World War. Of the 3,812 American casualties, many were members of the United States Army Air Corps, which held several bases in East Anglia. The site was donated by the University and dedicated on July 16, 1956. It is beautifully landscaped; set in open countryside, the headstones fan out in many concentric arcs revolving around a central flagpole. The Great Wall, bordering a pool edged with roses, records the names of The Missing and leads to the Memorial. This contains a chapel, a museum with a mosaic ceiling depicting an aircraft amidst mourning angels, and a wall carved with the campaign map.

ANDREW PEARCE

Andrew believes that the 'The early bird catches the worm'. He has been taking photographs of Cambridge for over 10 years and still enjoys discovering and photographing its hidden corners. He is an Associate of the Royal Photographic Society and his photography is often exhibited, and appreciated by the wider public on hand-made cards available in and around Cambridge.

CLAIRE DEVAS

Claire is a researcher, writer, and dedicated tourist. She was born in France and was a pupil at Bedales School before matriculating at Trinity College, Cambridge, where she gained a degree in French and Italian. She has worked extensively in the media industry, working for local and national newspapers, magazines, television and BBC Radio 4.

MIDSUMMER PUBLISHING

Midsummer Publishing was conceived from the view of Midsummer Common which I have the privilege to enjoy every day. I ended up here having had the good fortune to study Engineering at Emmanuel College, and seem to have stayed. For locals, Cambridge is a fantastic city to live in. It is calm and peaceful and has an plethora of places to appreciate. With this book, I hope that visitors will enjoy some of the things that we, the indigenous, have the pleasure of seeing every day.

Alan Martin

ACKNOWLEDGEMENTS

Special thanks to: Jeremy and Mary Martin; Johnny, Rachel and Fredi Devas; Lord St. John of Fawsley; Sonya Larkin; Brigid Martin; Katie Collins; Frances Lloyd; Andrew Garwood-Gowers; Emily Rogers; Andy Laing; Tom Rogers; Peter Garwood-Gowers; Rob Knight; Martine Parnell; Patrick McMahon; Sam Jones; Dunstan Bertshinger; Shoomon Perry; Peter Dawe; Wayne Lindsay; Patrick Conroy; Rob Walden.

Thanks for the expertise of: Chris Jakes: Cambridgeshire Collection; Margaret Greeves, The Fitwilliam Museum; Bob Headland and Lucy Martin, Scott Polar Research Institute; Becky Proctor, The Cambridgeshire Folk Museum; Catriona West, Whipple Museum; John Thompson; J.E.T Photographic; Phillip Mynott; George Swindle, Cambridge City Council.

Many thanks to The Master, bursar and fellows of the following colleges: Peterhouse; Clare; Corpus Christi; Gonville and Caius; Magdalene; King's; Queens'; Jesus; Christ's; St. John's; Trinity; Emmanuel; Sidney Sussex; Downing; Newnham.

BIBLIOGRAPHY

Bryan, Peter *Cambridge, The shaping of a city*

Casson, Hugh *Hugh Casson's Cambridge* (Phaidon Press Limited, London, 1998)

Ferguson, Douglas; Haycraft, Dona; Segal, Nick; *Cambridge* (Covent Garden Press, Cambridge, 1995)

Hall, Michael *Cambridge* (Pevensey Press, Cambridge, 2000)

Howard, Peter Webster, Helena *Cambridge an architectural guide (*Elipsis London Limited, London, 2000)

Jeacock, Janet *Cambridge Colleges*

Jeacock, Janet and Michael *Cambridge Official Guide* (Jarrold, Norwich, 2000)

Payne, Sara *Down Your Street I Central Cambridge* (Pevensey Press, Cambridge, 1983)

Payne, Sara *Down Your Street II East Cambridge* (Pevensey Press, Cambridge, 1984)

Robinson, Duncan *The Fitzwilliam Museum 1848-1998* (Fitzwilliam Museum, Cambridge, 1998)

www.cam.ac.uk

INDEX

The Wooden Bridge, Queens' College

FOLLOWING PAGE: *Cambridge Skies Over Schlumberger*